T0099745

Torn Together

L.J. Martin

authorHOUSE®

AuthorHouse™
1663 Liberty Drive
Bloomington, IN 47403
www.authorhouse.com
Phone: 1-800-839-8640

First published by AuthorHouse   3/22/2011

ISBN: 978-1-4567-2987-5 (e)
ISBN: 978-1-4567-2988-2 (sc)

Library of Congress Control Number: 2011901433

Printed in the United States of America

Any people depicted in stock imagery provided by Thinkstock are models,
and such images are being used for illustrative purposes only.
Certain stock imagery © Thinkstock.

This book is printed on acid-free paper.

Sending special hugs and kisses to my children. You are the most amazing inspiration, and source of unconditional love a mother could ever ask for. The most wonderful future awaits all three of you, got for it. You have already touched so many people's lives with your kindness, compassion and laughter.

To my family and friends for always being there, your faith in me was and continues to be a source of strength. You reminded me to never lose sight of what's really important in life and to never stop believing. I am truly blessed to have you in my life. Thank you.

Preface

This is to all people who are currently seeking a divorce, in a troubled relationship, or maybe it's just a thought that you should move on. Male or female, it's not an easy process. It certainly is not where I thought my marriage would end up. I grew up believing that marriage was forever. I was committed to it, believing it would never end. I knew it would have its ups and downs, but what I wasn't prepared for, was where to draw the line. How much trying, loving, patience, and forgiving is enough? These questions are highly personal and are up to you to answer. Only you can determine the breaking point or tolerance in your relationship. Each experience is unique and no less traumatic than the other. I hope in some way I accomplish bringing you to some conclusion as to where you need to be or where you need to go from here. Allowing strength, peace, and certainty of your own will to guide you in the most positive manner.

Writing A Book: Are You Kidding!

Of course as stated in the preface I want to reach out, be heard, and make a difference in your life. What self help book isn't after that, right?! Ironically I can't believe that I could or would write about a subject that has most likely hit epidemic proportions. It's not something I encourage, or want people to do. But I do want people to start thinking why we are making so many bad choices or putting ourselves in unhealthy relationships. We need to start making changes that are proactive or good choices in our future relationships.

So here I sit with pen in hand and a pile of notebook paper. (I wasn't always near a computer, so I carried this around when the flow of thought hit me.) I am dumbfounded that I am now a statistic for the records. My writing is a way to express my thoughts to you and share what has happened. It's my way to not only reach out to you, but somehow get through to you that any form of disrespect, not just physical, cannot and should not be tolerated. Any form of abuse (emotional, mental, physical), lying, cheating is not acceptable. If you think about it, respect is trusting, not hurting someone, and giving them your very best.

So here I go with my pen writing to you from the heart and a head reeling with thoughts to share with you. May the best of life come to you, a bright future to be lived. Always give a smile every day, even if it's not returned you may make someone's day without knowing it.

My Relationship Is Ok, Isn't It?

*B*eware, *maybe you think* your relationship is "OK", normal if you will. Most likely your idea of a good relationship was from observing your own parents growing up. Possibly you have observed over the years marriages from relatives, brothers, sisters, and close friends.

Does that make it okay if your marriage is just like one of theirs? Not if it's not healthy, filled with real love of give and take. Love that makes you know without a shadow of a doubt that your needs are the utmost importance to your partner and vice a versa.

Who Am I?

Who am I you ask? Nobody really, in the sense that "somebody" is well known by the public. I am simply a mother of three children, wife of a man who climbed the corporate ladder over the years with extensive travel, and long hours. Missing most of his children's milestones and certainly looking elsewhere for companionship other than home most likely. By trade I am a registered nurse. After the second child I stayed home because I felt these years could never be replaced or redone. I am glad I have done so. It took some sacrifice on the budget, but well worth being there for them.

Early in the marriage I accepted this lifestyle, of not having support or help at home. Did I like it, not really, but he wanted to make something of his life, so with my unconditional love I let him achieve his dreams. This was the way it was going to be, lonely, frustrating, and putting my goals and emotions to the side. I was just a homemaker now who was supposed to know not to cross the line of exerting too much independence, have too many problems, or say anything if he flirted or came onto other women.

Most of the time I was busy anyway, running the household, paying bills, taking kids to their activities, yard work etc. Just busy enough not to notice the loneliness or have enough energy to want to say anything.

As years went by that would change. I wanted a partner to talk to, to bounce ideas off of and troubleshoot with, not communicate to me like I was an employee with a task to complete for him.

Over the years I evolved into a person I scarcely knew. I was a competent woman, capable of handling what life had to throw at her, and a voice that wanted to be heard. A far cry from the person I was formally. The women who was quiet, subservient in a way, pleasing others hoping for acceptance or some form of recognition, was somehow transformed.

The Transformation

When I sat back and thought for a bit I realized I really liked the person I had become now. It was definitely a good and happy me. Possibly the Lord has intended for all of us to come to this realization and feel this way? It makes me sad to think how many of us don't come to this point or feel this way. Maybe beyond my wildest dreams this book will get to you and reach out to you with an understanding that you can be happy and move on. Or maybe you need to seek help with counseling etc. It really has to do with what you want to do with your behavior. Alter your life accordingly, with the more positive and content person you envision yourself being. I believe that bad things aren't the devil or anything else like that but of possibly of our own doing. We are creating what is happening around us daily and settling for relationships that aren't for us. We are just settling for whatever suits us for the moment, or tolerating the present situation, and not looking at the whole picture of the tomorrows we have. Think about it. Picture your marriage as it is right now, or the relationship you are in. How does it make you feel? Content and happy? Do you smile knowing that your thoughts, feelings and needs are being taken seriously by your mate? If the answer is no, then take time to evaluate your feelings. Imagine how it might be without the person creating these feelings for you. Does it feel better? Take time to really evaluate the possibilities. There will undoubtedly be good and bad to the new scenario, but most should point to a better feeling for you and the setbacks or financial changes certainly should be something that could be worked out. If you are free to finally be you and become happy again, I think anything is possible.

With all these factors in mind, I continue my story to you. Maybe it will spark something in you that you always felt but never dare try to be. I ask you, like I ask myself "what's the worst thing that could happen?" Possibly the old you was alright after all (we all make mistakes), a new found you, a realization that life has so much more to offer? Maybe more work or studying to be done so you can become the new and improved you. Gain independence in your existing situation or possibly break away into a new life for yourself. It's all ok I think as long as it moves you further to your dreams. Not trying gets you exactly "nowhere". So I'll try to reach out to you if you promise to at least step out of your comfort zone, even a little bit and better yourself. Free yourself if you will from a marriage/relationship that is not for you or maybe make your current situation work for you. No matter what, find you! This will mean you will like yourself and be happy with who you are, that's your first priority. After that you can enjoy life, and truly search for the good and right relationship you deserve!

Let's Start our Journey

Please keep in mind that I am not an expert. Not in relationships, psychotherapy, etc. I am just an ordinary mom of three great kids, who has been through a lot over the past few years. My kids are the thrust in my life, God gave me the privilege of having them and I intend to love them and raise them to the best of my abilities. Notice I didn't say it was easy! Raising kids is a daily challenge, especially when the home front is less than idyllic.

Just remember no home is perfect, honestly that perfect couple with the perfect house, kids, cute dog probably isn't as wonderful as you think.

What they do have, is two "willing" partners who know what it takes to keep a marriage together. Most likely they have trust, communicate well, have a sense of caring beyond themselves. It's the give and take theme. Maybe a loving relationship is nothing more than friendship intensified in a way.

I am honestly beginning to think it's not that easy to really find the perfect mate the first time around. Maybe most of us need that trial and error process to figure it all out? Some lucky few seem to find it early on, but I am beginning to think the majority of us don't. Keep in mind that past relationships can either leave you with painful baggage or a lot of helpful information for your future relationships. Simply put you can learn from your past or cry about it.

One thing I have tried to learn, (and repeat frequently!) it's OK to make mistakes. Even big ones, like marriage and divorce! What is life anyway I realized but a lesson to learn and grow from. It really is that simple.

If you aren't willing to move on "divorce" or seek help for a troubled marriage/relationship and grow from it, you have a long way to go. You're most likely destined for continued failure in your current relationship, or any future relationships. You will have many miserable days of wondering why this is happening to you, maybe hoping this will all go away, or that tomorrow will surely be better and different than before. It has to happen if you try hard enough to please the other person, right? They will surely change their ways or realize how miserable they are making you. You convince yourself time and time again, it will be different, it has to.

Plain and simple it's not going to happen. Trust me when I tell you, it won't change. I tried for 17years believing this had to work somehow. No one told me that pleasing another person really is being content and happy with yourself first. When you are happy it tends to lead to happier surroundings and better choices of people. Please realize that even with your positive changes, you cannot and will not change the other person-PERIOD. That is their lesson in life to learn, to be who they are and what they want to be. You shouldn't want to or need to change them anyway if he/she is the right one in your life. The right person will help you grow and want you to be happy and you should want this for them also. Yes, any good marriage/relationship will have bad days like everyone else. The difference lies in the ability to communicate and respect your mates feelings and move on after a disagreement/or argument. It should never lead to degrading, demeaning comments or bad feelings in any way. And it should not drag on for hours or days with mean looks or comments (this includes silence) that will continue to fuel the fight further. I can tell you personally it's the worst feeling to have to deal with. This is childish behavior, you're punishing your partner for trying to express themselves. This is not a healthy relationship, not to mention a bad example for your children to see. Now they are learning to communicate poorly and hold a grudge. You may see this show up with problems with their peers. They might have difficulty having and keeping friends. Please remember that an unhealthy marriage can affect everyone. This is really so important to keep in mind.

Personally my hardest part was accepting that I needed to move on, divorce my husband. Honestly it has taken me years battling my feelings to get to this point. I didn't want to accept the reality. For the longest time I didn't tell anyone in fear of rejection from family and or friends. The feeling persisted that somehow this was my fault. I had failed miserably at the one thing I cherished and looked forward to in life. For as long as I can remember I wanted a loving husband and kids to raise. Maybe I didn't do enough to save this marriage? Somehow I was embarrassed, I wanted to be happily married, not divorced. People will look at me differently. We won't be a couple anymore. Actually when news got out, some people did treat me differently. So be prepared for that possibility. The good news friends are friends no matter what. They were a great source of inspiration, as well as family, who listened tirelessly it seems on the bad days. If you don't have these resources, look for support groups, local churches or even a psychologist that will provide you with someone safe to listen and be there for you.

Once I dealt with these feelings (of my life changing-or knowing it had to), something happened. I realized I was embarrassed by my husband's actions. Once I accepted the reality that being disrespected at home and in public, being put down emotionally and sometimes physically abused was not OK, EVER.

I was empowered. Somehow I grew stronger than I had ever been before. Each day now is a new day to a new beginning, and a new adventure awaits. Why I was empowered this time or how this happened I can't really say for sure. These incidents had occurred for years, most of my marriage in fact. I do remember the incident that somehow was the last straw for me. The feeling came after he embarrassed me in public with the kids present and something inside me said "stop" enough is enough. He had flirted with a very young waitress (20 years my junior) and I leaned forward to try and join in the conversation, only to get glaring looks from both my husband and waitress to mind my own business. The kids innocently looked on watching this. I knew I didn't want to feel that way ever again. It was an overwhelming gut feeling. This was wrong for my kids to keep seeing bad behavior and I did not want them to repeat this with their potential mates one day. I kept thinking to myself, no one has a right to treat me this way because of their shortcomings, and that goes for you too. Your mate is supposed to build you up, not demean you or make you feel bad about yourself or life. This isn't what God intended for us, nor the life I envisioned.

I sat and thought, how did I get to this point? I realized it was years of burying my emotions at my expense, not his. I fed his ego, not mine. Personally, it's not healthy for any of us to do this. Myself I gained weight, became even more quiet, more withdrawn from family and friends. I didn't want to burden anyone with my problems or have to say how I was really being treated for fear of embarrassment as I stated above. I have always been the listener, helping everyone else. Guess who I forgot to listen to-myself.

My body and mind suffered. I can assure you prolonged stress will in some way affect you too. It has been well documented in the medical journals that prolonged stress can cause high blood pressure, lead to heart disease, weaken your immune system, cause depression and anxiety just to mention a few affects. I actually urge you to visit a doctor if you think you need help with your stress or emotions that seem overwhelming. It can actually kill you if left untreated to long.

Once I realized I was really stressed out I needed to figure out how to help myself. For myself I realized just getting out of the house and seeing friends I enjoy, have a great laugh, vent our frustrations and tell silly stories with one another was a good release for me. It's great fun and you don't feel so alone anymore. Exercise was the best way I found to get rid of excess feelings of anger, resentment, etc. Not to mention I am slowly losing weight along with a sensible diet. This was another boost to help me even feel better about myself and my situation. Each day started out as a baby step for me out of a comfort zone. Each step is a more positive feeling for me. I stay strong with a resolve toward happiness each day. I admit some day's I question is this the right thing to do? Not all days are easy to feel happy about! I just have to look forward to another day. Frequently I would ask myself, am I truly happy, fulfilled, content with where I am, and who I am with? The honest answer is "no" of course not. I remind myself to look forward not back and go for it.

For you the reader my advice is to find your "happy place" whether it be friends, family, exercise, going to the mall and just watching people and window shop. A good book store is always fun! Whatever is a healthy way for you to get rid of some pent up feelings and stress and start thinking clearly. Start it soon.

I think it's normal for any of us to question ourselves. Sometimes I take two steps back and evaluate how I feel being away from the current situation. Maybe you could even look at it as an outsider looking in. Concentrate on how the marriage/relationship is making you feel. Are you anxious, sad, confused, fearful. Do I really want these feelings on a daily basis. Of course not, we want a feeling of balance, happiness, and contentment with where life is going. What would you tell your friend to do? It's scary to leave our comfort zone, the familiar. Not to mention how in the world financially is this going to affect me. That scares me when I look at my three kids and wonder how can I possibly maintain a lifestyle similar to what they are used to, let alone college for three. I just have faith things will fall into place.

Poem

I am going to share with you a poem (or writing of feelings) that I wrote sometime in 2005 during some of my darkest days I guess. It's somewhat embarrassing to share my most intimate feelings with you, but if you feel something similar or understand in some way how I felt then maybe you will understand just how far I have come and realize you can too.

"Here I am. Darkness, it's all around. Everyone sees the nice house, cars, etc. It means nothing but emptiness. I live here in the dark, a big black hole where I can never reach the light. When I see a glimmer of light I reach out, even if it's a little bit, I try. Only to be tossed further into nothingness. My stomach burns like a pile of coals that were on fire all night, embers. My head aches constantly from the fight. The one who should hold me close to his chest or reach his hand out refuses to see, blind with hate of the whole ordeal, pushing me further until nothing but a shell will exist. I try hard every day to conquer it, to hide my pain, only to be sneered at, laughed at, misunderstood. Why?? I have only goodness in my heart, the love of the Lord, and yet he mocks me, lies, accuses me of so many untruths. Only the best of intentions are in my heart and life, only to be turned into the persons gain or ego. I hate the dark, it seems so endless and futile."

To clarify a bit, the mocking, laughing, lies were my husband after I would say how sad or lonely I felt in this relationship. He would stare out the window sometimes totally ignoring my existence. He was on his Blackberry constantly, then when he went to sleep he would hide hid Blackberry from me so I could never check it. Other times accusing me of affairs. I never touched another man let alone an affair. He would laugh at times telling me to get over whatever it was that bothered me. What bothered me most was a suspicion of his being with other women. Of course he denied for years of his infidelity. Later the truth of unfaithfulness came out.

In time I realized, these were signs and symptoms of his infidelity and guilt. For me mental and emotional abuse at it's worst. He had been projecting his insecurities and guilt and making them mine.

The Short or Long Way Out

Is a shorter process of divorce easier than a long drawn out one? Honestly I can't really say which way is better. Each brings it's own unique set of sequlae or outcome if you will. Mine has been long (somedays seemed like forever). My friend had it over in a matter of 12 weeks. Looking at it objectively, it seems the short divorce leaves gaps and unfinished business with feelings still buried. All must be dealt with for a better future and a foundation to a better relationship later on. You will find that you will have trust issues, or have difficulty believing fully in your next potential mate. If you have children, they will be left confused and scared as to what really happened. Children often blame themselves for the break up. In a later chapter I will explain the need for communication with your child/children. It's vital, a must for their well being. If you didn't communicate with them before, there's no better time than now! It heals and creates a trust/bond that both of you will need. I do want to briefly mention that a short divorce is probably needed in cases where you are not safe. This would include being married to an abusive person (emotional or physical), or someone involved in taking drugs or alcohol to the point of addiction and it alters who they are. In these cases, please seek a safe place for you and your child/children as soon as possible and see a lawyer for appropriate advice and action. For abuse you can always call 1-800-799-7233 which is the national domestic violence hotline.

For the long divorce, it obviously comes with prolonged stresses of back and forth with lawyers. What it does provide is time for everyone to think and adjust to the future possibilities. It will give the kids time to adjust to the idea of divorce and accept that changes will be coming and possibly have a say as to their preferences when possible (like where you can afford to live, give them a list of houses you like and let them choose their favorites , maybe they would like to stay at the same school with their friends etc) Sometimes it will give you time to settle volatile emotions down to an acceptable level and the terms of divorce can come to a more peaceful resolution. There are a myriad of emotions involved and hopefully you will take positive steps to make what most people make a terrible experience, and use it to your advantage for all parties involved.

No matter what your circumstances are, I can assure you of one fact, that it will be a virtual rollercoaster of emotion. Just know that the future is waiting for you to make the best of it, and you are in control of this. Remember strength is a choice, and your life is a choice. Write the last two sentences down and place near your bed or where you will see it often and read it when you are unsure or uneasy with what's happening. It will remind you that you are now in charge of your new future.

Feelings to Deal With

I suppose one of the biggest factors to deal with in relationships and divorce are feelings. Ours, theirs, the people involved around us.

Often I have asked myself if my marriage is "broken" do I fix it or get rid of it ? If you have tried various avenues, like marital counseling, seeking help at church, local groups etc. and you are getting nowhere, you have probably answered your own question!

An analogy for me in a troubled relationship would be like a wound a person would have. Do I bandage it (hide it so I don't see it) in hopes of healing and being like new again. Or am I just covering it up to not look at it more closely and have to deal with it or take care of it.

If I cover it up "bandage" without caring for it, this will cause possible inability to heal or fester an infection that is difficult, if not impossible to heal. Basically we are sweeping all the ugliness under the rug hoping it will all go away. Not tending to the problems (ugliness) will lead to deterioration. Every living thing, including humans need nurturing and to be cared for, or they eventually perish and fail to thrive.

I believe our feelings can play a large role in where one needs to be or where you end up. Remember as you read, strength is a choice. We will feel so many emotions through this process. I personally have felt sad, angry, mistrust, emptiness, self doubt. It's ok to feel all of these and more. But I always pull back to the feeling of wanting to feel good about myself and the life I want to create.

No matter the outcome you desire, remember that positive attitude and positive energy help create good choices and the best possible outcome. Now you are coming from a position of at least being happy. I believe good things will come from this way of thinking.

Someone who thinks and feels negative emotion will just project more negative outcomes and bad situations for themselves. You will come from a position of being sad and maybe even wonder why bad things keep happening to you. Think about it, nothing good can come from this point of view.

What it really comes down to is your circumstances are affected by what your behavior is. It's what you project or message you are sending out to others. Remember you cannot control the other persons behavior or thought process, but you most certainly can alter yours and feel good about who you are in this process. I want you the reader to feel good about yourself at the end of your relationship and/or divorce. I believe it is possible for this to happen. I'm doing my best to have this happen for myself, so can you.

Future Relationships

What does the future hold? It would be nice if we knew wouldn't it. Unfortunately we have to create our future. This time around I know I will personally take more time to see future relationships for what it has to bring and how it makes me feel. Keep in mind the first few months are a lot of fun and exciting "the honeymoon phase". Then reality comes into play and now is the time to evaluate how to function as a couple and accomplish everyday tasks. If you really want someone who likes to take charge and help you a lot, then please look for this and don't settle for someone who is just okay at handling things. This time have enough trust in yourself to insist that you are not interested in a long term relationship unless the person who brings out the very best in you and has your best interests at heart comes along. Otherwise being alone isn't so bad after all! It will take a lot of patience and faith, but I believe it can happen.

I think it would be helpful to make a list of traits you admire or like in a person. Be honest, dream big. Your list might look like this:

Appreciate/appealing traits/enjoy being around:

Dislike being around/turn offs/unappealing:

Don't just look at this list and admire it. Really know and believe you deserve this person. We should not settle for anyone less than what we expect this time. Let's learn from our mistakes and be thankful for knowing the difference.

Maybe a list of traits of the person you are leaving or had a bad relationship with could be helpful also. This way you can identify someone you know you shouldn't continue pursuing or get into a serious relationship with.

It would be a waste of your time after you struggled so hard to get away from the previous relationship to fall into a similar one that will only bring you down again. Gain strength by walking away and feel good about your choice to pursue an even better feeling relationship unlike anything you have had before. It's far easier to break up after a few months realizing that this isn't the person for you than continue on with false hope of changing someone or you are afraid of hurting their feelings.

Advice From Others

Undoubtedly when you start telling people you are getting a divorce, a plethora (meaning- many) of well meaning family members and friends will come forward. They will want to tell you what you should do or how you should be feeling. Many will have to share their own experiences with you or most certainly know someone who did and tell you about them!

It seems like common sense not to act on what they say to you, please remind yourself that every situation is unique in it's own way. So with that in mind, take the information you get as a tool to better help yourself if it applies to your situation. Some ideas will be helpful, others simply will not apply. You may end up with great ideas that you never thought of before. Keep in mind with stress we don't always think as clearly as we normally would.

Don't let anyone make you feel what you are doing is unjustified or wrong. They really don't know what you are personally experiencing. Words could never explain how trapped, scared, emotionally drained the other spouse has made you feel. Believe in yourself enough to take what they are saying lightly.

There are times when you may have to distance yourself from negative people. This may include family and or friends. Difficult as this is to do, it's in your best interest right now to eliminate anyone who makes life more stressful for you.

Let people in who are supportive, and caring. They should support you in the most positive manner to make the most difficult process a little less stressful.

Looking Back: Should I Have Known?

Should I have known from the beginning that my marriage was destined to fail? I suppose I did have some clues or insight. I should have paid more attention to his habits or preferences. Family values and how similar or dissimilar our upbringings were do make a difference. The old saying of you aren't marrying his family, well it does make a huge difference in how easy or hard it will be for you to have a healthy, productive marriage together.

Upon reflection I realized he was insecure in many ways. Anyone meeting him would never know this, he gave the appearance of confidence and strength. After time this insecurity and low self esteem turned into his wanting to be accepted (not just by me) but by actively flirting with other women. I even had someone call me after I got engaged and was told he would never be faithful to me. Possibly a clear warning he had a problem with long term commitments prior to me? I choose not to listen to the phone call. This was because we were very much in love. I thought she must be jealous! Maybe she had more insight than I realized? When I addressed the issue with him, he assured me those were silly, insignificant calls from his past and that he could never be unfaithful to me as his father had been so many times before to his mother. He shared how much it hurt him as a child watching the destructive behavior from his own father (his father had many affairs and was abusive), and he could never create that pain for his new wife and one day his own children.

Please look at the family. I know they say that you are not marrying the family, but I believe differently. Your potential mate received a majority of his relationship knowledge from this source. He/she observed on a daily basis on how to communicate (or not). Did he/she experience frequent arguments or fights within the family? Did they resolve the disagreements effectively and in a timely manner. Only the strong, self determined men or women seem to get beyond the dysfunctional family and mature into their own persons. They see their family as they truly are (dysfunctional), and strive for healthy relationships. Only a few lucky ones get it. Most continue with the same destructive and dysfunctional patterns observed. It is "normal" behavior to them because they have lived with it for so long and deny anything is wrong with them or their family. This will take years of therapy if they are ever willing to accept that there is a problem.

Please keep in mind that backgrounds that are similar will probably have a better chance at marriage. You will share common ways of thinking and beliefs that are close. I realize now that the person I chose to marry had a very different upbringing than I did and it became more prominent as the years went by. Instead of adopting our own way of life we would envision, it would constantly be a struggle. He often felt put down, I felt misunderstood. Neither one of us wanted to create these feelings, but it always ended up that way. We were both frustrated constantly trying to come up with a healthy way to get beyond these inadequacies and/or challenges of melding two different views or value systems into our own. The subjects ranged from how to raise the kids, how to care for personal items, cleanliness of the home, to comfort level of types of activities we liked to experience. He loved hype and crowds, I enjoy intimate groups of people and quite time. As time went on these differences did make it difficult, along with the other challenges we had to deal with.

There are definitely signs and characteristics in the mate you choose that should be looked at realistically. Over time the little things that kind of bother you may grow into big issues. If family is not supportive and helpful, they most likely won't be there when you hit a rough spot or need help in your marriage later on either.

Does your potential mate have a wandering eye? If so does it bother you, are you willing to accept this later on as the flirting becomes more intense as his/her needs by their standards are not being met and they need more attention outside the home.

No one can know for sure if their future mate is perfect for them, but I think looking more realistically and observing more closely than we might normally could be of use. There may be clues to patterns of behavior that may cause problems later on or different family values so far from your own that melding the two styles could prove to be an almost impossible task.

Maybe a longer engagement would be helpful to identify how all these dynamics work or don't work out?

Preparation for the Inevitable

As *silly as this* title may seem, you can position yourself before the papers are served. By position I mean to get your life in order so you can best protect yourself and your children's future. It will allow you to make better decisions when not in the throws of a heated divorce when stress and conflict are inevitable and we don't think as clearly. You will be able to plan for your life after divorce even though at times it will seem overwhelming. This process will hopefully make you feel better about the decision you have made and give you back control of your life.

If you don't have a credit card in your name only, I suggest getting at least one credit card in your name . This way you have credit started in your name only and have access to pay for bills should he/she pull financial means from you quickly. It is much easier for you to get a credit card married then after you are divorced. Make a few small purchases on your new card and pay them off each month to show you are of good standing to the creditors. This credit will also help you with future purchases like cars, homes, etc. Keep in mind divorce has a way of ruining ones credit. You may want get a free credit report to see where you stand. The legitimate companies never ask for your credit card. If your credit is poor, you may want to pay off some debt. If you have no credit for yourself you will find it very difficult to start a new life with no cash and no credit.

At this time make sure you do not take on anymore additional debt. For example, don't let your spouse talk you into refinancing the home, buy a new car you know you can't keep payments on afterwards. If your current car is questionable. Now is the time to have an inspection done and have repairs if needed. Costly repairs after the divorce can cause havoc with your new budget. This step will hopefully keep you going until you get your new budget in place after the divorce.

Most lawyers will tell you before papers are served to pull (withdraw) ½ of your savings and checking account. Put the money in another bank in your name only. Keep all receipts to prove when and how you moved the money so no questions are asked later. You can wait until this advice comes from your lawyer. Keep in mind that typically one needs 6 months worth of savings to plan ahead for the mortgage, bills, attorney fees, etc. should the spouse pull all the money. If you need or want to start your own account ahead of time without splitting the checking/ savings accounts and add to it slowly, this is another good option. Cut your grocery bill by 20-30 dollars each time and put in the new account. Think of clever ways you can pull just a little bit from usual expenses and put it away for the future. If you don't want the statements to come the house get a P.O. box. Please keep in mind that this money account is subject to division during the divorce. I have honestly had friends spouses get angry when papers were served, went to the bank and wiped out all accounts, including college money. None of us want to experience this, so be prepared. Keep all receipts for proof to your lawyer how these funds were being saved. You are looking out for your own interests and the children's at this point.

If you have any valuable jewelry, papers of importance, or anything of value that you wish not to disappear during the divorce coming up, once again I urge you to protect these and place in a secure spot. This could mean friends house, family, or your own safety deposit box. Claim it fairly in your divorce assets. If it was a gift then present it in the divorce papers that way, if it was bought during the marriage than you can both decide with the lawyers help how to split fairly. I add this part not to hide anything, but to have the items secure. These items could be taken out of anger by the other party and you are ensuring they will be fairly taken care of in the justice system. You may want to videotape your possessions, like the house contents, vehicles, anything of value to you.

Consider insurance next. If you are covered under your spouse's policy, go ahead and get complete medical and dental check-ups for you and the children. Most importantly if a problem is identified, have the procedure done now while you are covered. Seek out new health, automobile, home insurance premiums from various companies and compare them. Don't forget to include these new expenses into your post divorce budget if you are making one. For myself the kids will have medical coverage under my spouse, I have to cover myself which is costly.

Empower yourself as much as you can. Read and learn as much about the divorce law in your state. Each state varies with its requirements and statues. Statutes are laws passed or established by congress or state legislature. These seem to vary by state, so learn what you can on them. The internet is a powerful tool, use it. Books are great also.

When selecting a lawyer, ask around for referrals. Word of mouth is great for finding someone who is a great family law attorney. If you aren't sure then select a few you like (maybe 2-3) and make consultation appointments with each one. Please ask if they charge a fee for this. Some do charge for the initial consultation. Before speaking to a lawyer, make a list of questions. This will help you stay on track and be more efficient when you arrive. Keep in mind after the consult and you have selected your lawyer they charge by the hour. It usually isn't cheap!! (this should be one of your questions-how much per hour do you charge?) Some may charge even if you call on the phone for a question. Ask if they charge for email, as long as the emails aren't excessive or to frequent. Keep a running list of questions to keep the cost down. If you are wondering if I used these steps, the answer is absolutely. I even offered to copy a lot of the papers he needed in the beginning (financial), maybe you could do the same.

After you feel comfortable with your legal counsel, take time to put your records together for them. You will need record of names, DOB of each party and children. Account numbers, addresses and phone numbers of all your assets and debts. These would include your credit card companies, bank accounts, loans, stocks and bonds, mortgages, and title information. Provide tax statement for at least the last three years. Paystubs from each work place and employment information. If you have a business, provide a copy of your taxes for that, assets and debts associated with that business. You may need deeds, prenuptial agreements or any other agreements, wills, or power of attorney.

If you have an inheritance, make sure it is in your name only. Don't use it to buy marital property or use it to pay for marital expenses. Otherwise it will not be separate from the marital estate.

I personally kept a budget of income and expenses on Microsoft Office. This way I knew how much I was spending each month and how much I may need for support or alimony in the future. This was a help to my lawyer as he could easily see how my standard of living had been and the income I was provided. If you aren't so good at this you may have a family member help with this or hire a certified divorce financial planner.

Terms you should be familiar with during the divorce. You may hear "marital estate", this is everything that was acquired during the marriage. Your "net worth" is the total of all debts subtracted from the total value of your assets. The lawyer will have a worksheet for this, but it's nice to see what you have ahead of time.

Even though moving out of the house if tempting, don't do it. Check with your lawyer first about the legal implications. Especially if there is physical abuse, please ask your lawyer for sound advice. As I mentioned earlier, states have different laws. Some states you may hurt your chances of keeping your home or effect how the final custody will be decided.

I suppose this should go without saying. If you are separated or living separate lives, don't consider dating until the divorce is final. It will for sure anger your spouse making them less cooperative during the divorce. As I stated way in the beginning we want to get through this the best way possible with the least amount of resentment or hostility afterward.

Hopefully your future will seem better already, knowing you are taking steps to take care of yourself, and taking time to understand some of the laws in your state.

Are You Cheating?

With some thought I felt this chapter was needed since this is something that seems to happen often in marriages and undoubtedly happened in mine. I was blind at first as to the signs of unfaithfulness in my marriage. I can tell you the other person often makes you to feel you are the cause, the blame for their need to reach out. Please don't believe that for one minute. It is really their need to gain some kind of recognition or feeling of self worth that they are somehow lovable and likeable (they have low self esteem).

Below is a list to identify he/she may be having an affair.

1. Your spouse stops confiding in you or stops getting advice like they usually would, and becomes more quiet and resigned. They are almost a mystery at times, you try to figure out why they are so indifferent. You may feel the blame, like you did something to create their feelings or actions.

2. Mutual friends or co-workers act differently around you. They may know something or have heard through the grapevine stories of seeing the spouse out with someone different. Sometimes they may have heard stories how horrible you are, therefore justifying his/her behavior.

3. They have secretly set up a new email account.

4. Leaves the house smelling like they always do and coming home smelling different! Even scents on the shirt of perfume

or cologne. Obvious, but look for makeup or lipstick on the clothes,

5. They buy a cell phone without your knowledge.

6. May start sending the phone bill to the office address, especially after the bill had been sent to your house all along. Now they change it. (this happened to me)

7. They accuse you of not being faithful or they feel you are flirting too much. This is usually out of guilt from their behavior. They are very "accusatory" of your actions. (this happened to me also)

8. Starts exercising when they didn't have this behavior before, or joins a gym. (This helps their self image and hopefully attract the other person more).

9. They delete all incoming calls at home when they never did this before.

10. They delete all emails, incoming and sent, when they normally didn't have this pattern before.

11. Buys new clothes or underwear. For the female, she buys new bra/underwear or lingerie. (yes, indeed my husband bought a bunch of new Tommy Hillfinger underwear) For the lingerie, if you aren't seeing it in the bedroom, think about it.

12. The spouse who was once not helpful, starts being more into chores and pitching in. This has guilt written all over it. Or the other extreme of losing attention to the activities at home and or shows a definite change in attitude towards everyone in the house. (this occurred for me, he exhibited both behaviors at different times)

13. The spouse asks you to try new things in the bedroom or even asks to invite people into the relationship. (this one was tried on me also)

14. There may be a change in the pattern of sex. They either want it more often than usual, or they suddenly stop having

it with you as much. (I actually had him stop half way and say "you don't do it for me anymore" and walk away).

15. Works more than usual. This may include overtime, look at the paycheck for the overtime pay. Look at trips that are late into the evening or traveling more than previously. Also leaves earlier than needs to. (He definitely did this)

16. They may pick a fight or start something so they can leave the house.

17. May have taken a personal day or vacation day that wasn't with you. You will have to look for this.

18. He won't eat the dinner you prepared or even gets sick from your dinner. Well he ate at the other person's house! (Yep, he pushed a few dinners away)

19. Look at your bank accounts. Notice more money being taken out than is customary? Keep track. I actually made a spread sheet detailing money in and out. If I paid his work credit card, how much did I get in return. I found out it was never equal. He shorted me money most of the time. Also look at where the credit card charges are and the amount. Look for patterns and lunches for two. Any jewelry purchased you never saw? Hotels?

20. Your spouse may seem touchy or less comfortable around you. They anger more easily. In general they show erratic behavior patterns. As I stated earlier they may be hard to figure out.

21. This kind of goes with the gym one, but they are more into their appearance than they once were.

22. Shows sudden interest in new music, clothing styles, and different trends they didn't care about previously. (He tried wearing pucca beads which looked ridiculous for his age)

23. Spends more time on the internet than usual. Especially after you have gone to bed.

24. You get phone calls where the caller hangs up after they hear

your voice. (this happened a lot to me) He told me it was my imagination! Silly me!!

25. They don't respond to your phone calls, texts, or emails promptly as they used to. (their busy for heavens sake)

Basically it comes down to your gut feeling. You think it is innocent and they couldn't possibly be cheating on you. But deep down inside I knew (so will you) something wasn't right. He made me feel so many conflicting emotions with this part of our relationship. Because of the confusion and need to make sense of all this I became depressed. It took years for me to process and move beyond all this. I started gathering my own proof that my feelings were justified and real. The spreadsheets of missing money to putting all the signs I mentioned above together somehow starting making sense. If you need to ask the question in the first place "are you cheating" I think we have answered our own question.

If this issue is caught and addressed early, there may be hope for the marriage. The cheater needs therapy for sure with a licensed psychologist, psychiatrist, or family therapy practice who specializes in these matters.

After that you both should attend a marriage counselor together. This will hopefully bring all issues into the open and a better future for both of you.

If the truth of an affair is not dealt with soon after it occured or hidden for a long time it seems trust and the ability to lie easily(to my face) has a profound effect on the marriage and forgiveness factor. I may be able to forgive, but I had a real problem with trust after this. I actually asked him to help devise a plan or a way for me to gain trust in him again. This plan never came, nor did any communication. He simply stated I just needed to believe him that when he was out that's where he was and with whom he stated he was with. Hence my future awaits and I will move on. You can feel anyway you want. I personally had lost all faith in the one I loved the most. We now had no trust, respect was limited, and we weren't able to communicate effectively. To me these are big factors needed for a good marriage.

So Papers Are Served

Ready, set, go! Hopefully you have had time to think about how this will transpire and you have taken steps you need to ensure you will be alright during this process. I had a choice on where I could serve the papers, so be prepared for this option if it is presented to you. I could serve at home with the possibility of the kids being present or his workplace. Once again I was concerned about how this would affect him. I didn't want to cause him discomfort or embarrassment in front of his peers at work. The other option seemed less appealing since I am trying to keep routines and emotions as normal as possible. My downfall once again was concerning myself with his well being and how he is going to feel and not dealing with my own well being and emotional state. Quickly I reminded myself of this and thought rationally on the best option. Work was a safer alternative to home with kids present and hopefully diffuse any possible anger outbursts in front of them. Hopefully being served at work would give the spouse time to sit and think about what has just been presented and hopefully get a grip before coming home. Neither choice will be pleasant but know it is a step in the right direction for both parties involved. It has to be done.

Once the papers have been served get ready for even bigger swells of emotion. It is not an easy situation to be honest, especially if the person continues to reside in the same residence. You need to keep things as even keel and normal as possible, for yourself and most definitely the kids. Believe me when I say that this is a tall order when emotions are running high for both of you. Most days I am able to keep my composure when sharp words or looks come my way. I do admit there are days it's plain hard to do so. Just keep in mind the better you are at controlling your emotions and the situation the better off in court or mediation you will be. The spouse is most likely waiting for you to lose your temper or get physical so he/she can use it against you. Most things aren't certain, but I can guarantee that they will go running to their lawyer documenting any significant events between you or events occurring with the kids. Possibly they may even provoke this event if possible, please be aware not to succumb to their level and let them win. In the long run you will be rewarded for keeping your cool.

Maybe at this point I need to update you with my position of the long way or short way out! My divorce is taking quite a bit of time and I have to say it is mentally and physically draining me. But I still hold strong with my conviction to a better and freer life for myself and the kids. It will be worth it and I picture my life a year from now. How different it will be. Different stresses for sure, but ones I can conquer more easily without the disruption and foggy mind of a failing marriage. Along with more energy to pursue the goals I had set for myself. I look forward to feeling rested, healthier, and more able to create the life I had envisioned not so long ago.

Education and the Kids

I am a firm believer in education and intend to do the best to provide some, if not all assistance to get them all educated with a degree. Unless you have a child who is self motivated, I think it's our parental responsibility for at least 4 years of college or some type of certification to allow them a decent chance at life, and ability to care for themselves. It's my personal belief all children deserve this.

Children and Divorce

Explaining you are getting a divorce to your child/or children may be one of the most difficult and painful things you will have to do. I can tell you every time I thought I would break the news to them I would almost freeze. The words would not or could not come out! Looking at them trying to utter the words, I need to tell you something , "we have decided to get a divorce". You know how much confusion and pain this will cause them. Uttering these few words is heart wrenching for all concerned. You are telling the ones you love so much that the life they know now will be changing forever. Most likely in a big way.I struggled with my words, I wanted to make sure they understood one thing loud and clear. That none of this was their fault and we loved them so much, and nothing could ever change that.

During the divorce process I constantly reassured them everything would be alright now and in our new lives together. Even if we lived in two different places , we were still a family who loved them very much. It was hard knowing in my mind and heart that the child/children deserved none of this, not one bit. Like the divorce process itself you will go through absolute emotional turmoil, similar to the ones you are having about the divorce itself. I personally felt anxious (what do I say to them or how do I say the right thing), fearful (how do I tell them or when is the right time to tell them),guilty (I couldn't fix this somehow and avoid causing everyone further grief and pain).

The only thing I knew for sure was I needed to put my feelings and emotions aside for their benefit, which is not an easy thing to do when your emotions are all over the place. For me it was so important to reassure them life goes on after the divorce is final, and they will always be loved , cared for, and safe. In a positive manner I reassured them frequently during the process that we were there for them and their needs were important to us.

When you actually get to the point of telling them about the divorce and try to explain what happened, don't give huge details. I tried to use the simplest approach and tried telling them that we have been having problems which we seem not to be able to come to common ground with and feel it would be better if we tried a new way of living. Most likely your child/children have already figured out you were having difficulties and not getting along! Kids are perceptive and tune in more than we think. As I spoke to our kids, I let them know several times that this had nothing to do with them. I let them know that we have been having a hard time agreeing on key issues and after time this has created conflicts or bad feelings between us that we cannot fix. I did tell our kids (and you can to if they are old enough) that some of our disagreements or issues may have been about you, but in no way are you to blame or the cause of our problems. I continued telling them they had nothing to do with our inability to agree on the right bedtime or where they should sleep, whether you should play a certain sport, how we should or should not help with your homework. I know our kids heard us arguing these issues and of course other things also. But I really wanted them to know with all certainty that we were never fighting or disagreeing about them. It really is mom and dad's difficulty in agreeing or seeing eye to eye on these issues. I wanted them to see the difference of why they were not to blame or how it was not their fault. It just simply wasn't true. It was our inability to come to terms or agree with one another.

As our divorce progressed, I continued to let them know that mom will always be mom and dad will always be dad. We will always be your parents, and no one can ever change that. I told them we both love them and we will always be there for them, even as our lives continue to change. As silly as this sounds I think they needed to hear this.

I honestly wish there wasn't a word "divorce". It seems so scary to all parties involved. You know when you hear this word your life will forever be changed. Frequently I had to remind myself that change is okay and then I reminded the kids the same thing. Change is okay and life is really just a series of changes if you think about it. Explain to the kids that with change things will be different in some way for sure. Not all the changes we will have during the divorce or even life in general will be perfect or positive. We need to do our best to adjust, learn and grow from this. It's an important lesson for all of us to learn to adjust to changes in our life and willingly accept them as a normal progression of life (keep in mind my kids were older so they were able to get this-you may have to be more simple for your child/children's age). I talked to them about how many things have already changed in our lives. Here are some examples of what we discussed in the car, or at the dinner table. I reminded them each year they go to a new grade in school. You have a new teacher, usually they have new students to get to know, and how nervous and scared they were the first day or two. They agreed after a couple of days it wasn't as bad as they thought, and most times it was a positive good change they ended up enjoying. Another example was starting a new sport for the first time. They were never sure they were capable of playing the sport, and I always heard " I don't know the coach or the kids I am with". Once again after chatting they realized how all these ended up being fun, exciting, good experiences and they always made new friends. They were glad they had tried something new. So we all agreed changes give us a way to do new things. Maybe even for the better sometimes. Maybe we could be happier in two different homes, where we could all be more peaceful and calm. These changes are not about who's right or wrong, or who's bad or good. I told them dad and I both tried our best to resolve our problems and differences. It didn't work for us, so now we are going to try this way for our family. Even though we are all uncertain of what these changes may be yet, it seems things always work out. I assured them we will get used to these changes in our lives, we may have new schedules, some new responsibilities. In time I am hoping we will all look back and say, life is definitely different then it was, but it is actually okay. Or maybe even better than we could have imagined?!

I am including a little humorous story to remind us all to choose our words carefully. Remember a child's mind does not think like we do, so think before you speak on how they will interrupt our words.

The Good Napkins

My mother taught me to read when I was four years old (her first mistake). One day, I was in the bathroom and noticed one of the cabinet doors was ajar. I read to box in the cabinet. I then asked my mother why she was keeping "napkins" in the bathroom. Didn't they belong in the kitchen?

Not wanting to burden me with unnecessary facts, she told me that those were for "special occasions" (her second mistake).

Now fast forward a few months….It's Thanksgiving Day, and my folks are leaving to pick up my uncle and his wife for dinner. Mom had assignments for all of us while they were gone. Mine was to set the table.

When they returned, my uncle came in first and immediately burst into laughter. Next came his wife who gasped, then began giggling. Next came my father, who roared with laughter. Then came Mom, who almost died of embarrassment when she saw each place setting on the table with a "special occasion" Kotex napkin at each plate, with the fork carefully arranged on top. I had even tucked the little tail in so they didn't hang off the edge.

My mother asked me why I used these and, of course, my response sent the other adults into further fits of laughter.

"But Mom, you said they were for special occasions!!!"

My Daughters' Perspective of Divorce:

Through time what's hidden from view comes to sight but comes ever so slowly like rain falling in a drought. Over time I learned what you know is different from what you can believe, even in your own family. However everything and everybody was torn together so I had to see through that and find hope between lies, lost expectations, trauma, and fighting.

Looking into someone's eyes, someone you've known since birth, and not knowing how they felt, thought, or acted, affected me. Tears fell onto the floor from my hazel eyes. I was lost in a world like most Americans I was living through my parents' divorce. I was as scared as a newborn baby.

Before when I was 5 everything was under control and proper. My family worked together, shared ideas and experiences, and was well-rounded. If we had a question we asked each other. We trusted and cared for each other. We were a family. I loved it that way until I realized my family was breaking down over time and the family split apart.

I was impacted so much that I relied on myself for answers. I knew if I asked somebody a question like how will we make it or what will we do the words would somehow hurt me no matter how pleasant they were. I couldn't stand life itself because it didn't make sense.

Now I know not only did my world change, but all the small things that didn't seem to matter made the bigger picture. Over the course of the 2 years we sold our house, got rid of our cats, and got a new smaller car. More importantly, I was graduating elementary school and merging into middle school dramatically fast.

Furthermore for me looking farther into the situation seemed better because I got a feel of the world around me making me judge it as stability. After a while I realized through that sense of stability I couldn't settle with a solid answer because everything changed before my eyes, nothing stayed the same. Everything changed to fast. Every day I had something bigger to distinguish. My world was in a haze.

All throughout the time I was hearing muffled words. Words I didn't understand. The words of hatred, deception, and rage. It wouldn't have affected me as much as it did if it didn't come out of my father's mouth. It put me back in my shell. I lost hope in who I was and who I was going to be.

I changed remarkably in those years. Touching the wood of my old house for the last time, smelling the last juicy burger made on our old grill, to being able to taste the tension in the air helped me grow so much just by moving on. Through that time I learned that everything can fall apart even without you doing a thing. But the true ending factor is that you will be ok no matter what. What you know is different from what you can believe. Now and forever I know that through everything you just have to believe so you won't be torn together.

So How Does This End?

I guess the obvious statement is no matter the circumstances as to our relationship difficulties, actually ending the marriage or relationship will be the hardest thing to do. Even though mentally I knew (and you will to) it needed to be done and it was the best option for all parties involved. For me it was a painfully long decision from the break up to the actual divorce. It took me literally years justifying to myself I wasn't happy and knowing something wasn't right (the affairs for me was just a gut feeling but couldn't prove for a long time). Of course my becoming unhappy and unsettled feeling fueled and justified his lying and cheating further. These last few years I have spent trying to become a happier person, resolute that these changes I desired (divorce and moving on with life) knowing they needed to occur, no matter what! I came to the realization that no matter how I tried to change my behavior for my husband to be happy, it really did not fix his perceived pain or lack. I knew I could only really control how I wanted to feel and be, which was to be a person who was in control of her life and to be happy. To do this I worked at more improved feelings within myself each day until I truly felt happy again. If I spent my energy or thoughts on his lack or sadness, I always felt bad, because I could not change this. This was for him to handle and for him to find within himself.

My personal belief is to take some time to feel good about yourself before you actually start the divorce or leave. Then evaluate how, when you want to start this process. Leaving feeling angry, guilty, or defensive will make it difficult to have a productive divorce for all parties and will probably lead to further replay of what you just left in future relationships. You can't find closure or peace with this scenario. There are instances as I mentioned before where the marriage or relationship is not appropriate to continue, if there is drug, alcohol, or abuse. Then leaving as soon as possible is the best choice.

If you think about it when you leave unhappy you are really taking yourself (the unhappy person) with. You may feel some relief from the intensity of the unhappiness and discord that you were experiencing. I can almost guarantee after a short time you will start justifying to yourself why you left (probably over and over) and how miserable you were. What happens is you end up in a continual state of still being unhappy. So now think about it, I just walked away from an unpleasant situation that bothered me, and guess what, I am still bothered and not happy.

Once again, the toughest part may be deciding when and how to end it. But before you do this, deal with your feelings to get to a better emotional place. It's hard when you look back and know how much you believed this was forever. You trusted your feelings for this person. You had faith in your relationship, your partner, and your ability that together you could get through anything life threw at you as a couple. To make matters even more difficult, now you may have a child or children, property, assests to contend with. Once the reality sets in that everything you had faith in and believed in was not what you expected and you tried everything, you think now what?! Some people stay in these bad relationships far to long. Others die in them, never leaving the bad situation. Statistically even people in abusive relationships go back time after time. For me none of these were options I could live with.

I feel we all deserve to move on and find true happiness. Somehow down the road I think we will be thankful for this, that we had the strength to change our selves for the better and our lives.

It's a step by step process it seems. Though I cannot tell you how many steps it takes or any short cuts to the end. There's no formula or foolproof way that tells us that it's time to leave or end it. I really think it's as individual as we are. I think mentally I left in every way possible many times before I physically decided it was time to move on.

Keep in mind it's okay if you do not share your true intentions or thoughts about leaving with anyone. I realized myself if I finally said I was leaving, everyone would constantly remind me or question, "I thought you were leaving" " Are you still leaving" . It was a gradual process of accepting things myself before sharing and committing to this divorce.

I will share with you something personal that my husband never understood and made comments about. We tried a marriage counselor, someone he had been seeing on his own for a few visits before I went. I agreed to try as I wanted this to work out. Once I went I never wanted to go back. I could never explain to anyone that I realized after that visit I had already lost faith in my husband and our relationship. It didn't happen overnight I realized, but this had been years of broken promises that he will try to change, that he will stop flirting in front of the kids and I, that we could come first (not work), he would be home more, and put his Blackberry down where it was accessible for me to see so we could build trust again. You simply don't care anymore whether it works or not. I didn't even care by the end whose fault it was. I just wanted out of this dreadful, unhappy, relationship. I wanted to be free with the new mentally and physically better and happy me.

I personally take responsibility for any mistakes I made, I am not perfect. I forgive others for theirs. These admissions do not mean that I have to live with this person anymore. You weigh your options , what are we willing to sacrifice to gain freedom. I did this in private, with determination, and a lot of patience. I did it this way trying not to hurt or affect the people involved as little as possible.

Remember be true to you, stay positive, and live healthy. There is no time limit on how long it takes to decide to leave. The choice is yours to change your mind however many times you want to, it's okay and it's normal. It certainly doesn't make us less of a person who is weak or indecisive. I think it means we are doing the right thing that matters to us. I have faith that you'll know when you are ready.

Quote "A woman has got to love a bad man once or twice in her life, to be thankful for a good one" Margorie Kinnan Rawlings.

To The Reader

Remember the biggest stumbling block is our selves. With this in mind, this is my wish for each and every one of you.

May today there be peace within. May you trust in yourself, and not forget the infinite possibilities that are born in all of us. May you use these gifts that you have received, and pass on the love and kindness that has been given to you. May you be content with yourself, just the way you are. Let this knowledge settle into your bones, and allow your soul the freedom to sing, dance, praise, and love. It's there for each and every one of us.